Lemon Recipe

By Carla Hutson

Table of Contents

Lemon Garlic Roasted Chicken

Introduction: Lemon-garlic roasted Chicken is a classic dish that combines the bright flavors of lemon and the aromatic essence of garlic to create a mouthwatering and comforting meal. This recipe yields tender and juicy chicken with crispy golden skin infused with the tangy zest of lemon and the savory richness of garlic. Perfect for a family dinner or special occasion, this roasted chicken is sure to be a crowd-pleaser.

Prep Time: 10 minutes Cook Time: 1 hour 20 minutes Total Time: 1 hour 30 minutes

Ingredients:

- ✓ 1 whole chicken (about 4-5 pounds)
- ✓ Salt and pepper to taste
- ✓ 2 lemons, sliced
- ✓ 6 cloves garlic, minced
- ✓ 2 tablespoons olive oil
- ✓ 1 teaspoon dried thyme
- ✓ 1 teaspoon dried rosemary
- ✓ 1 teaspoon dried oregano
- ✓ 1/2 teaspoon paprika
- ✓ Fresh parsley for garnish (optional)

Method:

1. Preheat your oven to 375°F (190°C).
2. Rinse the chicken inside and out under cold running water, then pat dry with paper towels. Season the chicken generously with salt and pepper inside the cavity and on the skin.
3. In a small bowl, combine the minced garlic, olive oil, dried thyme, rosemary, oregano, and paprika to make the lemon garlic herb rub.
4. Gently loosen the chicken's skin by carefully sliding your fingers between the skin and the meat. Be careful not to tear the skin.
5. Rub the lemon garlic herb mixture under the chicken's skin, spreading it evenly over the breast and thigh meat.
6. Stuff the cavity of the chicken with lemon slices and any remaining garlic cloves.

7. Tie the chicken's legs together with kitchen twine and tuck the wing tips under the chicken's body.

8. Place the chicken breast on a roasting rack inside a roasting pan.

9. Roast the chicken in the preheated oven for about 1 hour and 20 minutes, or until the internal temperature reaches 165°F (75°C) in the thickest part of the thigh and the juices run clear.

10. Once cooked, remove the chicken from the oven and let it rest for 10-15 minutes before carving.

11. If desired, garnish with fresh parsley and serve the Lemon Garlic Roasted Chicken with your favorite sides.

12. Enjoy the tender and flavorful chicken infused with the zesty essence of lemon and aromatic garlic!

Lemon Blueberry Pancakes

Lemon Blueberry Pancakes are a delightful twist on the classic breakfast favorite, combining the bright citrus flavor of lemon with the sweetness of juicy blueberries. These fluffy pancakes are perfect for a leisurely weekend brunch or any morning when you want to start your day on a delicious note. Drizzle with maple syrup and enjoy the burst of flavor in every bite!

Prep Time: 10 minutes Cook Time: 15 minutes Total Time: 25 minutes

Ingredients:

- ✓ 1 cup all-purpose flour
- ✓ 2 tablespoons granulated sugar
- ✓ 1 teaspoon baking powder
- ✓ 1/2 teaspoon baking soda
- ✓ 1/4 teaspoon salt
- ✓ 1 cup buttermilk
- ✓ 1 large egg
- ✓ Zest of 1 lemon
- ✓ 2 tablespoons fresh lemon juice
- ✓ 1/2 teaspoon vanilla extract
- ✓ 1 cup fresh blueberries
- ✓ Butter or oil for greasing the griddle or skillet

Method:

1. Whisk the flour, sugar, baking powder, baking soda, and salt in a large mixing bowl.
2. In a separate bowl, whisk together the buttermilk, egg, lemon zest, lemon juice, and vanilla extract until well combined.
3. Pour the wet ingredients into the dry ingredients and stir until combined. Be careful not to overmix; a few lumps in the batter are okay.
4. Gently fold in the fresh blueberries.
5. Preheat a griddle or non-stick skillet over medium heat and lightly grease with butter or oil.

6. Pour 1/4 cup of batter onto the preheated griddle for each pancake, spacing them apart to allow room for spreading.
7. Cook the pancakes for 2-3 minutes on the first side or until bubbles form on the surface and the edges appear set.
8. Flip the pancakes and cook for 1-2 minutes on the second side until golden brown and cooked through.
9. Repeat with the remaining batter, adjusting the heat to prevent burning.
10. Serve the Lemon Blueberry Pancakes warm with maple syrup, additional fresh blueberries, and a sprinkle of lemon zest, if desired.
11. Enjoy these fluffy and flavorful pancakes bursting with the perfect balance of lemon and blueberry!

Lemon Butter Shrimp Pasta

Lemon Butter Shrimp Pasta is a quick and elegant dish that combines succulent shrimp with a luxurious lemon butter sauce, served over a bed of tender pasta. This recipe is perfect for busy weeknights or special occasions when you want to impress your family or guests with a delicious and satisfying meal. You can create a restaurant-worthy dish with just a few simple ingredients that will surely become a favorite.

Prep Time: 10 minutes Cook Time: 15 minutes Total Time: 25 minutes

Ingredients:

- ✓ 8 oz linguine or your favorite pasta
- ✓ 1 lb large shrimp, peeled and deveined
- ✓ Salt and pepper to taste
- ✓ 2 tablespoons olive oil
- ✓ 4 tablespoons unsalted butter
- ✓ 4 cloves garlic, minced
- ✓ Zest of 1 lemon
- ✓ Juice of 1 lemon
- ✓ 1/4 cup chopped fresh parsley
- ✓ Grated Parmesan cheese for serving (optional)

Method:

1. Cook the pasta according to the package instructions until al dente. Drain and set aside, reserving 1/2 cup of pasta water.
2. Season the shrimp with salt and pepper to taste.
3. Heat the olive oil in a large skillet over medium-high heat. Add the shrimp and cook for 2-3 minutes on each side or until they are pink and opaque. Remove the shrimp from the skillet and set aside.
4. Melt the butter in the same skillet over medium heat. Add the minced garlic and cook for 1-2 minutes, or until fragrant.
5. Add the lemon zest and juice to the skillet, stirring to combine.
6. Return the cooked shrimp to the skillet and toss to coat in the lemon butter sauce.

7. Add the cooked pasta and chopped parsley to the skillet, tossing until the pasta is evenly coated in the sauce. If the sauce is too thick, add some reserved pasta water to loosen it up.
8. Season with additional salt and pepper to taste, if needed.
9. If desired, Serve the Lemon Butter Shrimp Pasta hot, garnished with grated Parmesan cheese.
10. Enjoy this delicious and flavorful pasta dish featuring succulent shrimp in a tangy lemon butter sauce!

Lemon Poppy Seed Muffins

Lemon Poppy Seed Muffins are a delightful treat that combines the bright citrus flavor of lemon with the nutty crunch of poppy seeds. These moist and tender muffins are perfect for breakfast, brunch, or as a sweet snack any time of day. Bursting with lemony goodness and speckled with poppy seeds, these muffins will brighten your day with their refreshing flavor.

Prep Time: 15 minutes Cook Time: 18-20 minutes Total Time: 35 minutes

Ingredients:

- ✓ 2 cups all-purpose flour
- ✓ 3/4 cup granulated sugar
- ✓ 2 teaspoons baking powder
- ✓ 1/4 teaspoon baking soda
- ✓ 1/4 teaspoon salt
- ✓ Zest of 2 lemons
- ✓ 1/4 cup fresh lemon juice
- ✓ 1/2 cup unsalted butter, melted and cooled
- ✓ 2/3 cup milk
- ✓ 2 large eggs
- ✓ 1 teaspoon vanilla extract
- ✓ 2 tablespoons poppy seeds

Method:

1. Preheat your oven to 375°F (190°C). Line a 12-cup muffin tin with paper liners or grease with non-stick cooking spray.
2. In a large mixing bowl, whisk the flour, sugar, baking powder, baking soda, salt, and lemon zest until well combined.
3. In a separate bowl, whisk together the melted butter, lemon juice, milk, eggs, and vanilla extract until smooth.
4. Pour the wet ingredients into the dry ingredients and stir until combined. Be careful not to overmix; a few lumps in the batter are okay.
5. Gently fold in the poppy seeds until evenly distributed throughout the batter.

6. Divide the batter evenly among the prepared muffin cups, filling each cup about 2/3 full.
7. Bake in the oven for 18-20 minutes until the muffins are golden brown and a toothpick inserted into the center comes clean.
8. Remove the muffins from the oven and let them cool in the tin for 5 minutes before transferring to a wire rack to cool completely.
9. Once cooled, serve the Lemon Poppy Seed Muffins and enjoy the bright and flavorful combination of lemon and poppy seeds!

Lemon Herb Roasted Vegetables

Lemon Herb Roasted Vegetables is a vibrant and flavorful side dish showcasing seasonal vegetables' natural sweetness paired with the fresh zest of lemon and aromatic herbs. This recipe is incredibly versatile and allows you to use a variety of your favorite vegetables, making it perfect for using up whatever you have on hand. Whether served as a side dish for a holiday meal or as a nutritious addition to your weeknight dinner, these roasted vegetables will surely be a hit with your family and friends.

Prep Time: 15 minutes Cook Time: 25-30 minutes Total Time: 40-45 minutes

Ingredients:

- ✓ 4 cups mixed vegetables (such as carrots, potatoes, bell peppers, zucchini, and cherry tomatoes), chopped into bite-sized pieces
- ✓ 2 tablespoons olive oil
- ✓ Zest of 1 lemon
- ✓ 2 tablespoons fresh lemon juice
- ✓ 2 cloves garlic, minced
- ✓ 1 teaspoon dried thyme
- ✓ 1 teaspoon dried rosemary
- ✓ 1 teaspoon dried oregano
- ✓ Salt and pepper to taste
- ✓ Fresh parsley for garnish (optional)

Method:

1. Preheat your oven to 400°F (200°C). Line a large baking sheet with parchment paper or aluminum foil for easy cleanup.
2. In a large mixing bowl, combine the chopped vegetables, olive oil, lemon zest, lemon juice, minced garlic, dried thyme, rosemary, oregano, salt, and pepper. Toss until the vegetables are evenly coated with the seasoning mixture.
3. Spread the seasoned vegetables in a single layer on the prepared baking sheet, ensuring they are not crowded to allow for even roasting.

4. Roast in the preheated oven for 25-30 minutes, or until the vegetables are tender and golden brown, stirring halfway through the cooking time to ensure even browning.
5. Once the vegetables are roasted to perfection, remove them from the oven and transfer to a serving dish.
6. Garnish with fresh parsley, if desired, and serve the Lemon Herb Roasted Vegetables hot as a delicious and nutritious side dish.
7. Enjoy the vibrant flavors of lemon and herbs infused into tender roasted vegetables!

Lemon Ricotta Pancakes

Lemon Ricotta Pancakes are a decadent twist on the classic breakfast favorite, featuring fluffy pancakes infused with the creamy richness of ricotta cheese and the bright citrus flavor of lemon. These pancakes are light, airy, and irresistibly delicious, perfect for a special weekend brunch or any morning when you want to treat yourself to something extraordinary.

Prep Time: 10 minutes Cook Time: 10 minutes Total Time: 20 minutes

Ingredients:

- ✓ 1 cup all-purpose flour
- ✓ 2 tablespoons granulated sugar
- ✓ 1 teaspoon baking powder
- ✓ 1/2 teaspoon baking soda
- ✓ 1/4 teaspoon salt
- ✓ 1 cup ricotta cheese
- ✓ 2 large eggs
- ✓ 1/2 cup milk
- ✓ Zest of 1 lemon
- ✓ 2 tablespoons fresh lemon juice
- ✓ Butter or oil for greasing the griddle or skillet
- ✓ Maple syrup and fresh berries for serving (optional)

Method:

1. Whisk the flour, sugar, baking powder, baking soda, and salt in a large mixing bowl.
2. whisk together the ricotta cheese, eggs, milk, lemon zest, and lemon juice in a separate bowl until smooth.
3. Pour the wet ingredients into the dry ingredients and stir until combined. Be careful not to overmix; a few lumps in the batter are okay.
4. Preheat a griddle or non-stick skillet over medium heat and lightly grease with butter or oil.
5. Pour 1/4 cup of batter onto the preheated griddle for each pancake, spacing them apart to allow room for spreading.

6. Cook the pancakes for 2-3 minutes on the first side or until bubbles form on the surface and the edges appear set.
7. Flip the pancakes and cook for 1-2 minutes on the second side until golden brown and cooked through.
8. Repeat with the remaining batter, adjusting the heat to prevent burning.
9. If desired, Serve the Lemon Ricotta Pancakes warm with maple syrup and fresh berries.
10. Enjoy these light and fluffy pancakes infused with the creamy richness of ricotta cheese and the vibrant flavor of lemon!

Lemon Garlic Butter Salmon

Lemon Garlic Butter Salmon is an elegant and flavorful dish featuring tender salmon fillets in a rich and tangy lemon garlic butter sauce. This recipe is quick and easy to prepare, making it perfect for busy weeknights or special occasions when you want to impress your family or guests with a delicious and nutritious meal. Serve the Lemon Garlic Butter Salmon with your favorite side dishes for a complete and satisfying dinner.

Prep Time: 10 minutes Cook Time: 10 minutes Total Time: 20 minutes

Ingredients:

- ✓ 4 salmon fillets (about 6 oz each), skin-on or skinless
- ✓ Salt and pepper to taste
- ✓ 2 tablespoons unsalted butter
- ✓ 3 cloves garlic, minced
- ✓ Zest of 1 lemon
- ✓ Juice of 1 lemon
- ✓ 2 tablespoons chopped fresh parsley
- ✓ Lemon slices for garnish (optional)

Method:

1. Season the salmon fillets with salt and pepper to taste on both sides.
2. Melt the butter in a large skillet over medium heat. Add the minced garlic and cook for 1-2 minutes or until fragrant.
3. Add the salmon fillets to the skillet, skin-side down if using skin-on fillets, and cook for 4-5 minutes.
4. Carefully flip the salmon fillets and continue to cook for 3-4 minutes, or until the salmon is cooked to your desired doneness and flakes easily with a fork.
5. During the last minute of cooking, add the lemon zest, lemon juice, and chopped parsley to the skillet, spooning the lemon garlic butter sauce over the salmon.
6. Once cooked, remove the salmon fillets from the skillet and transfer to a serving platter.

7. If desired, garnish with lemon slices and drizzle with any remaining lemon garlic butter sauce from the skillet.
8. Serve the Lemon Garlic Butter Salmon immediately with your favorite side dishes.
9. Enjoy the succulent salmon fillets bathed in a tangy lemon garlic butter sauce!

Lemon Rosemary Roast Chicken

Lemon Rosemary Roast Chicken is a classic, comforting dish perfect for any occasion, from a cozy family dinner to a festive holiday meal. Tender and juicy chicken is infused with the vibrant flavors of fresh lemon and aromatic rosemary, resulting in a mouthwatering main course that will impress. This simple yet elegant recipe requires minimal preparation and always yields delicious results.

Prep Time: 15 minutes Cook Time: 1 hour 15 minutes Total Time: 1 hour 30 minutes

Ingredients:

- ✓ 1 whole chicken (about 4-5 pounds)
- ✓ Salt and pepper to taste
- ✓ 2 tablespoons olive oil
- ✓ Zest of 1 lemon
- ✓ Juice of 1 lemon
- ✓ 3-4 cloves garlic, minced
- ✓ 2 tablespoons fresh rosemary, chopped
- ✓ Lemon slices for garnish (optional)
- ✓ Fresh rosemary sprigs for garnish (optional)

Method:

1. Preheat your oven to 375°F (190°C). Place a roasting rack inside a roasting pan or large baking dish.
2. Rinse the chicken under cold water and pat dry with paper towels. Season the chicken generously with salt and pepper, both inside and out.
3. To make the marinade, combine the olive oil, lemon zest, lemon juice, minced garlic, and chopped rosemary in a small bowl.
4. Rub the marinade all over the chicken, making sure to coat both the exterior and the cavity.
5. Place the chicken breast on the roasting rack in the prepared pan. Tuck the wing tips under the chicken's body and tie the legs together with kitchen twine, if desired, to help the chicken cook evenly.

6. Arrange lemon slices on top of the chicken and, if using, place a few rosemary sprigs in the cavity for additional flavor and aroma.

7. Roast the chicken in the oven for approximately 1 hour and 15 minutes, or until the internal temperature reaches 165°F (75°C) and the juices run clear when pierced with a knife. If the skin starts to brown too quickly, tent the chicken with aluminum foil halfway through the cooking time.

8. Once cooked, remove the chicken from the oven and let it rest for 10-15 minutes before carving.

9. Carve the Lemon Rosemary Roast Chicken into serving portions and garnish with additional lemon slices and fresh rosemary sprigs, if desired.

10. Serve the succulent roast chicken hot with your favorite side dishes.

11. Enjoy the tender and flavorful Lemon Rosemary Roast Chicken with your family and friends!

Lemon Thyme Roasted Potatoes

Lemon Thyme Roasted Potatoes are a simple yet flavorful side dish that pairs perfectly with various main courses. Tender baby potatoes are roasted to golden perfection with fresh lemon, aromatic thyme, and garlic, resulting in a comforting and satisfying dish. These roasted potatoes are easy to prepare and make a delicious addition to any meal, from weeknight dinners to holiday feasts.

Prep Time: 10 minutes Cook Time: 30-35 minutes Total Time: 40-45 minutes

Ingredients:

- ✓ 1.5 pounds baby potatoes, halved or quartered if large
- ✓ 2 tablespoons olive oil
- ✓ Zest of 1 lemon
- ✓ Juice of 1 lemon
- ✓ 2 cloves garlic, minced
- ✓ 1 tablespoon fresh thyme leaves
- ✓ Salt and pepper to taste
- ✓ Fresh thyme sprigs for garnish (optional)

Method:

1. Preheat your oven to 425°F (220°C). Line a baking sheet with parchment paper for easy cleanup.
2. In a large mixing bowl, toss the halved baby potatoes with olive oil, lemon zest, lemon juice, minced garlic, fresh thyme leaves, salt, and pepper until evenly coated.
3. Spread the seasoned potatoes in a single layer on the prepared baking sheet, ensuring they are not overcrowded to ensure even roasting.
4. Roast the potatoes in the oven for 30-35 minutes, or until golden brown and crispy on the outside and tender on the inside, stirring halfway through the cooking time for even browning.
5. Once perfectly roasted, remove the potatoes from the oven and transfer to a serving dish.

6. If desired, garnish with fresh thyme sprigs and serve the Lemon Thyme Roasted Potatoes hot as a delicious and satisfying side dish.
7. Enjoy the irresistible combination of tender roasted potatoes infused with the bright flavors of lemon and thyme!

Lemon Basil Pesto Pasta

Lemon Basil Pesto Pasta is a vibrant and flavorful dish celebrating basil and lemon's fresh and fragrant combination. This pasta dish is simple yet elegant, perfect for weeknight dinners and special occasions. The homemade basil pesto is brightened with the zest and juice of fresh lemon, creating a sauce that is light, refreshing, and irresistibly delicious. Tossed with your favorite pasta and topped with Parmesan cheese, this Lemon Basil Pesto Pasta will surely become a new favorite in your recipe rotation.

Prep Time: 15 minutes Cook Time: 10 minutes Total Time: 25 minutes

Ingredients:

- ✓ 8 ounces (about 225 grams) pasta of your choice (such as spaghetti, linguine, or penne)
- ✓ 2 cups fresh basil leaves, packed
- ✓ 1/2 cup grated Parmesan cheese, plus extra for serving
- ✓ 1/3 cup pine nuts or walnuts
- ✓ 2 cloves garlic, peeled
- ✓ Zest of 1 lemon
- ✓ Juice of 1 lemon
- ✓ 1/2 cup extra-virgin olive oil
- ✓ Salt and pepper to taste
- ✓ Fresh basil leaves and lemon slices for garnish (optional)

Method:

1. Cook the pasta according to the instructions in a large pot of salted boiling water until al dente. Reserve 1/2 cup of pasta cooking water, then drain the pasta and set aside.
2. While the pasta is cooking, prepare the basil pesto. Combine the fresh basil leaves, grated Parmesan cheese, pine nuts or walnuts, garlic cloves, lemon zest, and lemon juice in a food processor or blender.
3. Pulse the ingredients until coarsely chopped, then gradually add the extra-virgin olive oil in a steady stream while the processor runs until the pesto is smooth and well combined. If the pesto is too thick,

add some reserved pasta cooking water to reach your desired consistency.

4. Season the basil pesto with salt and pepper to taste, and adjust the lemon juice or zest if desired for a brighter flavor.
5. In a large mixing bowl, toss the cooked pasta with the prepared lemon basil pesto until evenly coated.
6. Serve the Lemon Basil Pesto Pasta hot, garnished with extra grated Parmesan cheese, fresh basil leaves, and lemon slices if desired.
7. Enjoy this vibrant and flavorful pasta dish as a delicious and satisfying meal!

Lemon Garlic Butter Scallops

These lemon garlic butter scallops are a delightful combination of tender scallops cooked to perfection in a flavorful lemon garlic butter sauce.

Prep Time: 10 minutes Cook Time: 10 minutes Total Time: 20 minutes

Ingredients:

- ✓ 1 pound scallops, rinsed and patted dry
- ✓ Salt and pepper to taste
- ✓ 2 tablespoons unsalted butter
- ✓ 2 tablespoons olive oil
- ✓ 4 cloves garlic, minced
- ✓ Zest of 1 lemon
- ✓ Juice of 1 lemon
- ✓ 2 tablespoons chopped fresh parsley

Method:

1. Season the scallops with salt and pepper on both sides.
2. Heat the butter and olive oil in a large skillet over medium-high heat until the butter is melted and foamy.
3. Add the minced garlic to the skillet and sauté for about 1 minute until fragrant.
4. Add the scallops to the skillet in a single layer, ensuring not to overcrowd the pan. Cook for 2-3 minutes on each side until golden brown is cooked through.
5. Remove the scallops from the skillet and set aside.
6. Add lemon zest, juice, and chopped parsley to the skillet. Stir well to combine and let it simmer for another minute.
7. Return the scallops to the skillet and toss to coat them evenly with the lemon garlic butter sauce.
8. Remove from heat and serve the scallops immediately, garnished with additional parsley if desired.

Lemon Raspberry Cheesecake Bars

These lemon raspberry cheesecake bars are a delightful combination of tangy lemon, sweet raspberries, and creamy cheesecake on a buttery crust.

Prep Time: 20 minutes Cook Time: 40 minutes Chilling Time: 4 hours Total Time: 5 hours

Ingredients:

- ✓ 1 1/2 cups graham cracker crumbs
- ✓ 1/4 cup granulated sugar
- ✓ 1/2 cup unsalted butter, melted
- ✓ 16 ounces cream cheese, softened
- ✓ 1/2 cup granulated sugar
- ✓ 2 large eggs
- ✓ 1 teaspoon vanilla extract
- ✓ Zest of 1 lemon
- ✓ 1/4 cup fresh lemon juice
- ✓ 1 cup fresh raspberries

Method:

1. Preheat the oven to 350°F (175°C). Grease a 9x13-inch baking dish and line it with parchment paper, leaving an overhang for easy removal.
2. combine the graham cracker crumbs, 1/4 cup sugar, and melted butter in a bowl. Press the mixture into the bottom of the prepared baking dish.
3. In another bowl, beat the cream cheese and 1/2 cup sugar until smooth and creamy. Add the eggs one at a time, beating well after each addition. Mix in the vanilla extract, lemon zest, and lemon juice until combined.
4. Pour the cream cheese mixture over the crust and spread it evenly.
5. Drop spoonfuls of raspberry preserves onto the cheesecake layer. Use a knife to gently swirl the preserves into the cheesecake batter.
6. Bake for 35-40 minutes or until the edges are set and the center is slightly jiggly.

7. Remove from the oven and let it cool completely in the pan on a wire rack.
8. Once cooled, refrigerate for at least 4 hours or until firm.
9. Using the parchment paper overhang, lift the cheesecake bars from the pan. Cut into squares and serve chilled. Enjoy!
10. I'll provide the recipes for the remaining dishes shortly!

Lemon Garlic Butter Asparagus

This lemon garlic butter asparagus recipe combines the vibrant flavors of lemon and garlic with tender-crisp asparagus spears, making it a perfect side dish for any meal.

Prep Time: 5 minutes Cook Time: 10 minutes Total Time: 15 minutes

Ingredients:

- ✓ 1 pound asparagus, woody ends trimmed
- ✓ 2 tablespoons unsalted butter
- ✓ 2 cloves garlic, minced
- ✓ Zest of 1 lemon
- ✓ Juice of 1/2 lemon
- ✓ Salt and pepper to taste
- ✓ Grated Parmesan cheese (optional)

Method:

1. In a large skillet, melt the butter over medium heat.
2. Add minced garlic to the skillet and sauté for about 1 minute until fragrant.
3. Add the trimmed asparagus spears to the skillet. Season with salt and pepper.
4. Cook the asparagus for 5-7 minutes, stirring occasionally, until tender but still crisp.
5. Add lemon zest and lemon juice to the skillet. Toss the asparagus to coat evenly with the lemon garlic butter sauce.
6. Remove from heat and transfer the asparagus to a serving dish.
7. Optionally, sprinkle grated Parmesan cheese over the asparagus before serving.
8. Serve the lemon garlic butter asparagus hot as a delightful side dish.

Lemon Dill Salmon Burgers

These lemon dill salmon burgers are packed with flavor from fresh herbs and zesty lemon, making them a delicious and healthy alternative to traditional beef burgers.

Prep Time: 15 minutes Cook Time: 10 minutes Total Time: 25 minutes

Ingredients:

- ✓ 1 pound fresh salmon fillet, skin removed
- ✓ 2 tablespoons fresh dill, chopped
- ✓ Zest of 1 lemon
- ✓ 1 tablespoon lemon juice
- ✓ 2 green onions, finely chopped
- ✓ 1/2 cup breadcrumbs
- ✓ 1 egg
- ✓ Salt and pepper to taste
- ✓ Olive oil for cooking
- ✓ Burger buns and toppings of choice (lettuce, tomato, avocado, etc.)

Method:

1. Cut the salmon fillet into small pieces and place them in a food processor.
2. Add chopped dill, lemon zest, lemon juice, green onions, breadcrumbs, egg, salt, and pepper to the food processor.
3. Pulse the mixture until well combined but still slightly chunky.
4. Divide the salmon mixture into 4 equal portions and shape them into burger patties.
5. Heat olive oil in a skillet over medium-high heat.
6. Cook the salmon burgers for 4-5 minutes on each side or until golden brown is cooked through.
7. Toast the burger buns if desired.
8. Assemble the burgers by placing the salmon patties on the buns and adding your favorite toppings.
9. Serve the lemon dill salmon burgers hot with lemon wedges.

Lemon Parmesan Roasted Brussels Sprouts

These lemon parmesan roasted Brussels sprouts are crispy on the outside, tender on the inside, and bursting with flavor from lemon and Parmesan cheese.

Prep Time: 10 minutes Cook Time: 25 minutes Total Time: 35 minutes

Ingredients:

- ✓ 1 pound Brussels sprouts, trimmed and halved
- ✓ 2 tablespoons olive oil
- ✓ Zest of 1 lemon
- ✓ Juice of 1/2 lemon
- ✓ 1/4 cup grated Parmesan cheese
- ✓ Salt and pepper to taste
- ✓ Red pepper flakes (optional)

Method:

1. Preheat the oven to 400°F (200°C). Line a baking sheet with parchment paper.
2. In a bowl, toss the Brussels sprouts with olive oil, lemon zest, lemon juice, grated Parmesan cheese, salt, pepper, and red pepper flakes (if using).
3. Spread the Brussels sprouts on the prepared baking sheet in a single layer.
4. Roast in the preheated oven for about 20-25 minutes or until golden brown and crispy, stirring halfway through.
5. Remove from the oven and transfer the roasted Brussels sprouts to a serving dish.
6. Sprinkle with additional grated Parmesan cheese if desired.
7. Serve the lemon Parmesan roasted Brussels sprouts hot as a delicious side dish.

Lemon Honey Glazed Carrots

Lemon Honey Glazed Carrots are a delightful side dish that brings flavor to any meal. The natural sweetness of carrots is enhanced by a tangy lemon-honey glaze, creating a perfect balance of flavors. This dish is simple to prepare yet impressive enough to serve at special occasions or holiday gatherings. With just a few ingredients and minimal effort, you can enjoy these tender and flavorful glazed carrots as a delicious accompaniment to your favorite dishes.

Prep Time: 10 minutes Cook Time: 15 minutes Total Time: 25 minutes

Ingredients:

✓ 1 pound (about 450 grams) carrots, peeled and sliced into rounds
✓ 2 tablespoons unsalted butter
✓ 2 tablespoons honey
✓ Zest of 1 lemon
✓ Juice of 1 lemon
✓ Salt and pepper to taste
✓ Chopped fresh parsley for garnish (optional)

Method:

1. Melt the butter over medium heat in a large skillet or saucepan.
2. Add the sliced carrots to the skillet and cook, stirring occasionally, for 5-7 minutes or until slightly softened.
3. In a small bowl, whisk together the honey, lemon zest, and lemon juice until well combined.
4. Pour the honey-lemon mixture over the carrots in the skillet and toss to coat evenly.
5. Reduce the heat to medium-low and continue to cook the carrots for an additional 5-8 minutes, stirring occasionally, until they are tender and glazed.
6. Season the glazed carrots with salt and pepper to taste, adjusting the seasoning as needed.
7. Remove the skillet from the heat Once the carrots are cooked to your liking and coated in the lemon-honey glaze.

8. Transfer the Lemon Honey Glazed Carrots to a serving dish and garnish with chopped fresh parsley, if desired, for a pop of color and freshness.
9. Serve the glazed carrots hot as a delicious and vibrant side dish that complements any meal.
10. Enjoy the tender and flavorful Lemon Honey Glazed Carrots with your family and friends!

Lemon Pepper Chicken Wings

Lemon Pepper Chicken Wings are a zesty and flavorful appetizer sure to please a crowd. These wings are seasoned with a tangy lemon pepper seasoning blend and baked to crispy perfection in the oven. Whether you're hosting a game day party or simply craving a tasty snack, these Lemon Pepper Chicken Wings are a delicious choice that will leave everyone wanting more.

Prep Time: 10 minutes Cook Time: 45 minutes Total Time: 55 minutes

Ingredients:

- ✓ 2 pounds (about 900 grams) chicken wings, split at the joint, tips removed
- ✓ 2 tablespoons olive oil
- ✓ Zest of 1 lemon
- ✓ Juice of 1 lemon
- ✓ 1 tablespoon lemon pepper seasoning
- ✓ 1 teaspoon garlic powder
- ✓ 1 teaspoon onion powder
- ✓ 1/2 teaspoon salt
- ✓ 1/4 teaspoon black pepper
- ✓ Lemon wedges and chopped fresh parsley for garnish (optional)

Method:

1. Preheat your oven to 400°F (200°C). Line a baking sheet with parchment paper or aluminum foil for easy cleanup.
2. In a large mixing bowl, toss the chicken wings with olive oil, lemon zest, lemon juice, lemon pepper seasoning, garlic powder, onion powder, salt, and black pepper until evenly coated.
3. Arrange the seasoned chicken wings in a single layer on the prepared baking sheet, spacing them apart to ensure even cooking.
4. Bake the chicken wings in the oven for 40-45 minutes or until golden brown and crispy, flipping halfway through the cooking time for even browning.

5. Once the Lemon Pepper Chicken Wings are perfect, remove them from the oven and transfer to a serving platter.
6. If desired, garnish with lemon wedges and chopped fresh parsley for extra flavor and freshness.
7. Serve the crispy and flavorful Lemon Pepper Chicken Wings hot as a crowd-pleasing appetizer or snack.
8. Enjoy these zesty wings with your favorite dipping sauce or as is for a burst of lemony goodness!

Lemon Blueberry Bread

This Lemon Blueberry Bread is a delightful combination of tart lemon and sweet blueberries, all wrapped up in a moist and tender loaf. Perfect for breakfast, brunch, or a sweet snack any time of day.

Prep Time: 15 minutes Cook Time: 1 hour Total Time: 1 hour 15 minutes

Ingredients:

- ✓ 1/2 cup unsalted butter, softened
- ✓ 1 cup granulated sugar
- ✓ 2 large eggs
- ✓ 1/2 cup plain Greek yogurt
- ✓ Zest and juice of 1 lemon
- ✓ 1 1/2 cups all-purpose flour
- ✓ 1 teaspoon baking powder
- ✓ 1/4 teaspoon baking soda
- ✓ 1/4 teaspoon salt
- ✓ 1 cup fresh blueberries

Method:

1. Preheat the oven to 350°F (175°C). Grease and flour a 9x5 inch loaf pan.
2. In a large bowl, cream the softened butter and sugar until light and fluffy.
3. Beat the eggs one at a time, then stir in the Greek yogurt, lemon zest, and lemon juice until well combined.
4. whisk together the flour, baking powder, baking soda, and salt in a separate bowl.
5. Gradually add the dry ingredients to the wet ingredients, mixing until combined. Be careful not to overmix.
6. Gently fold the fresh blueberries until evenly distributed throughout the batter.
7. Pour the batter into the prepared loaf pan and spread it into an even layer.

8. Bake in the oven for 55-65 minutes or until a toothpick inserted into the center comes clean.
9. Remove the bread from the oven and let it cool in the pan for 10 minutes, then transfer it to a wire rack to cool completely.
10. Once cooled, slice the lemon blueberry bread and serve. Enjoy!

Lemon Garlic Butter Shrimp Skewers

These Lemon Garlic Butter Shrimp Skewers are a simple yet elegant dish perfect for summer grilling. Succulent shrimp are marinated in a flavorful lemon garlic butter sauce and grilled to perfection. Serve them as an appetizer or main course for a delicious seafood feast.

Prep Time: 15 minutes Cook Time: 6 minutes Total Time: 21 minutes (plus marinating time)

Ingredients:

- ✓ 1 pound large shrimp, peeled and deveined
- ✓ 4 cloves garlic, minced
- ✓ Zest and juice of 1 lemon
- ✓ 1/4 cup unsalted butter, melted
- ✓ 2 tablespoons chopped fresh parsley
- ✓ Salt and pepper to taste
- ✓ Wooden skewers, soaked in water for 30 minutes

Method:

1. In a large bowl, whisk together the minced garlic, lemon zest, lemon juice, melted butter, chopped parsley, salt, and pepper to make the marinade.
2. Add the peeled and deveined shrimp to the marinade and toss to coat evenly. Cover and refrigerate for at least 30 minutes to allow the flavors to meld.
3. Preheat the grill to medium-high heat.
4. Thread the marinated shrimp onto the soaked wooden skewers, dividing evenly.
5. Grill the shrimp skewers on each side for 2-3 minutes until they are pink and opaque.
6. Remove the shrimp skewers from the grill and transfer them to a serving platter.
7. Garnish with additional chopped parsley and lemon wedges if desired, then serve immediately. Enjoy!

Lemon Herb Quinoa Salad

This Lemon Herb Quinoa Salad is light and refreshing, packed with nutritious ingredients and vibrant flavors. With fluffy quinoa, crunchy vegetables, and a zesty lemon herb dressing, it's perfect for a healthy lunch or side dish.

Prep Time: 15 minutes Cook Time: 15 minutes Total Time: 30 minutes

Ingredients:

- ✓ 1 cup quinoa, rinsed
- ✓ 2 cups water or vegetable broth
- ✓ 1 cup cherry tomatoes, halved
- ✓ 1 cucumber, diced
- ✓ 1/2 cup red onion, finely chopped
- ✓ 1/4 cup fresh parsley, chopped
- ✓ 1/4 cup fresh mint, chopped
- ✓ Zest and juice of 1 lemon
- ✓ 2 tablespoons olive oil
- ✓ Salt and pepper to taste

Method:

1. bring the water or vegetable broth to a boil in a medium saucepan. Stir in the quinoa, then reduce the heat to low, cover, and simmer for 15 minutes, or until the quinoa is cooked and the liquid is absorbed.
2. Remove the cooked quinoa from the heat and let it cool to room temperature.
3. combine the cooked quinoa, halved cherry tomatoes, diced cucumber, finely chopped red onion, chopped parsley, and chopped mint in a large bowl.
4. To make the dressing, whisk together the lemon zest, lemon juice, olive oil, salt, and pepper in a small bowl.
5. Pour the dressing over the quinoa salad and toss until evenly coated.
6. Taste and adjust the seasoning as needed.

Lemon Garlic Butter Green Beans

These Lemon Garlic Butter Green Beans are a simple yet flavorful side dish that pairs perfectly with any meal. Tender green beans are sautéed in a garlic-infused lemon butter sauce, creating a bright, fresh, and delicious dish.

Prep Time: 10 minutes Cook Time: 10 minutes Total Time: 20 minutes

Ingredients:

- ✓ 1 pound fresh green beans, trimmed
- ✓ 2 tablespoons unsalted butter
- ✓ 2 cloves garlic, minced
- ✓ Zest and juice of 1 lemon
- ✓ Salt and pepper to taste
- ✓ Chopped fresh parsley for garnish (optional)

Method:

1. Bring a large pot of salted water to a boil. Add the green beans and cook for 2-3 minutes or until they are bright green and tender. Drain the green beans and set aside.
2. Melt the butter in a large skillet over medium heat. Add the minced garlic and cook for 1-2 minutes or until fragrant.
3. Add the cooked green beans to the skillet along with the lemon zest and lemon juice. Toss to coat the green beans in the lemon garlic butter sauce.
4. Cook for 2-3 minutes, stirring occasionally, until the green beans are heated and coated in the sauce.
5. Season with salt and pepper to taste, then transfer the green beans to a serving dish.
6. Garnish with chopped fresh parsley if desired, then serve immediately. Enjoy!

Lemon Coconut Energy Balls

These Lemon Coconut Energy Balls are the perfect healthy snack to satisfy your sweet cravings. Made with simple ingredients like dates, almonds, coconut, and lemon zest, these no-bake energy balls are packed with flavor and nutrition to energize you throughout the day.

Prep Time: 15 minutes Chill Time: 30 minutes Total Time: 45 minutes

Ingredients:

- ✓ 1 cup pitted dates
- ✓ 1 cup raw almonds
- ✓ 1/2 cup shredded coconut, plus extra for rolling
- ✓ Zest of 1 lemon
- ✓ 2 tablespoons lemon juice
- ✓ 1 tablespoon water (if needed)

Method:

1. combine the pitted dates, raw almonds, shredded coconut, lemon zest, and lemon juice in a food processor. Pulse until the mixture comes together and forms a sticky dough. If the mixture is too dry, add water, 1 tablespoon at a time, until it reaches the desired consistency.
2. Scoop out tablespoon-sized portions of the dough and roll them into balls between your palms.
3. Roll the energy balls in additional shredded coconut to coat them evenly.
4. Place the coated energy balls on a baking sheet lined with parchment paper.
5. Chill the energy balls in the refrigerator for 30 minutes to firm up.
6. Once chilled, transfer the energy balls to an airtight container and store them in the refrigerator for up to 2 weeks.
7. Enjoy these Lemon Coconut Energy Balls as a quick and nutritious snack anytime you need an energy boost!

Lemon Garlic Roasted Broccoli

This Lemon Garlic Roasted Broccoli is a simple yet flavorful side dish that will elevate any meal. Tender broccoli florets are roasted to perfection with garlic, lemon zest, and lemon juice, creating a bright, zesty, and irresistibly delicious dish.

Prep Time: 10 minutes Cook Time: 20 minutes Total Time: 30 minutes

Ingredients:

- ✓ 1 pound broccoli florets
- ✓ 2 tablespoons olive oil
- ✓ 4 cloves garlic, minced
- ✓ Zest of 1 lemon
- ✓ Juice of 1 lemon
- ✓ Salt and pepper to taste
- ✓ Grated Parmesan cheese for garnish (optional)

Method:

1. Preheat the oven to 425°F (220°C). Line a baking sheet with parchment paper.
2. In a large bowl, toss the broccoli florets with olive oil, minced garlic, lemon zest, lemon juice, salt, and pepper until evenly coated.
3. Spread the seasoned broccoli florets in a single layer on the prepared baking sheet.
4. Roast in the oven for 15-20 minutes or until the broccoli is tender and slightly caramelized around the edges.
5. Remove from the oven and transfer the roasted broccoli to a serving dish.
6. Garnish with grated Parmesan cheese if desired, then serve immediately. Enjoy!

Lemon Pepper Grilled Chicken

This Lemon Pepper Grilled Chicken is a simple and flavorful dish perfect for summer cookouts or weeknight dinners. The chicken is marinated in a zesty lemon pepper marinade and then grilled to juicy perfection, resulting in tender and delicious chicken with a hint of citrus and spice.

Prep Time: 10 minutes Marinating Time: 1 hour Cook Time: 12 minutes Total Time: 1 hour 22 minutes

Ingredients:

- ✓ 4 boneless, skinless chicken breasts
- ✓ 1/4 cup olive oil
- ✓ Zest and juice of 2 lemons
- ✓ 2 cloves garlic, minced
- ✓ 2 teaspoons lemon pepper seasoning
- ✓ 1 teaspoon salt
- ✓ 1/2 teaspoon black pepper
- ✓ Chopped fresh parsley for garnish (optional)
- ✓ Lemon wedges for serving

Method:

1. To make the marinade, whisk together the olive oil, lemon zest, lemon juice, minced garlic, lemon pepper seasoning, salt, and black pepper in a small bowl.
2. Place the chicken breasts in a shallow dish or resealable plastic bag and pour the marinade over them. Make sure the chicken is evenly coated. Cover the dish or seal the bag and refrigerate for at least 1 hour or overnight for best results.
3. Preheat the grill to medium-high heat.
4. Remove the chicken breasts from the marinade and discard any excess marinade.
5. Grill the chicken breasts on each side for 6-7 minutes until they are cooked through and have grill marks.
6. Remove the chicken from the grill and let it rest for a few minutes before slicing.

7. If desired, garnish the grilled chicken with chopped fresh parsley and serve with lemon wedges on the side for squeezing over the chicken. Enjoy!

Lemon Cream Cheese Pound Cake

This Lemon Cream Cheese Pound Cake is a rich and indulgent dessert with a lemon flavor. Moist and tender, with a velvety texture, it is made even more decadent with cream cheese. Perfect for any occasion, from afternoon tea to dessert after dinner.

Prep Time: 20 minutes Bake Time: 1 hour 10 minutes Total Time: 1 hour 30 minutes

Ingredients:

- ✓ 1 cup unsalted butter, softened
- ✓ 8 ounces cream cheese, softened
- ✓ 2 cups granulated sugar
- ✓ 4 large eggs
- ✓ 1 teaspoon vanilla extract
- ✓ Zest and juice of 2 lemons
- ✓ 3 cups all-purpose flour
- ✓ 1/2 teaspoon baking powder
- ✓ 1/2 teaspoon salt
- ✓ Powdered sugar for dusting (optional)

Method:

1. Preheat the oven to 325°F (160°C). Grease and flour a 10-inch bundt pan.
2. In a large bowl, cream the softened butter, softened cream cheese, and granulated sugar until light and fluffy.
3. Beat the eggs individually, then stir in the vanilla extract, lemon zest, and lemon juice.
4. sift together the flour, baking powder, and salt in a separate bowl.
5. Gradually add the dry ingredients to the wet ingredients, mixing until combined. Be careful not to overmix.
6. Pour the batter into the prepared bundt pan and spread it into an even layer.
7. Bake in the preheated oven for 1 to 1 hour 10 minutes, or until a toothpick inserted into the center comes out clean.

8. Remove the cake from the oven and let it cool in the pan for 10 minutes, then transfer it to a wire rack to cool completely.
9. Once cooled, dust the lemon cream cheese pound cake with powdered sugar before serving, if desired. Enjoy!

Lemon Garlic Butter Artichokes

These Lemon Garlic Butter Artichokes are a delicious and elegant appetizer or side dish perfect for special occasions or everyday meals. Tender artichoke hearts are steamed until tender, then drizzled with a flavorful lemon garlic butter sauce that takes them to the next level.

Prep Time: 10 minutes Cook Time: 30 minutes Total Time: 40 minutes

Ingredients:

- ✓ 4 large artichokes
- ✓ 1 lemon, halved
- ✓ 4 tablespoons unsalted butter
- ✓ 4 cloves garlic, minced
- ✓ Salt and pepper to taste
- ✓ Chopped fresh parsley for garnish (optional)

Method:

1. Trim the stems and tops of the artichokes, then remove any tough outer leaves. Use kitchen shears to trim the sharp points off the remaining leaves.
2. Fill a large pot with about 2 inches of water. Squeeze the juice from one-half of the lemon into the water and add the lemon half to the pot.
3. Place a steamer basket in the pot and arrange the artichokes in the basket.
4. Cover the pot and bring the water to a boil. Reduce the heat to medium-low and let the artichokes steam for 25-30 minutes, or until the outer leaves pull off easily and the base is tender when pierced with a knife.
5. While the artichokes are steaming, melt the butter in a small saucepan over medium heat. Add the minced garlic and cook for 1-2 minutes or until fragrant. Remove from heat and set aside.
6. Once the artichokes are cooked, remove them from the steamer basket and transfer them to a serving platter.

7. Cut the remaining lemon half into wedges. Squeeze some lemon juice over the steamed artichokes, then drizzle them with the garlic butter sauce.

8. Season with salt and pepper to taste, then garnish with chopped fresh parsley if desired.

9. Serve the lemon garlic butter artichokes warm or at room temperature, with extra lemon wedges on the side for squeezing. Enjoy!

Lemon Herb Grilled Lamb Chops

These Lemon Herb Grilled Lamb Chops are a delightful dish perfect for a special dinner or a backyard barbecue. The tender lamb chops are marinated in a flavorful mixture of lemon, garlic, and herbs and then grilled to perfection, resulting in juicy and flavorful chops that are sure to impress.

Prep Time: 10 minutes Marinating Time: 1 hour Cook Time: 10 minutes Total Time: 1 hour 20 minutes

Ingredients:

- ✓ 8 lamb chops
- ✓ Zest and juice of 2 lemons
- ✓ 4 cloves garlic, minced
- ✓ 2 tablespoons chopped fresh rosemary
- ✓ 2 tablespoons chopped fresh thyme
- ✓ 1/4 cup olive oil
- ✓ Salt and pepper to taste
- ✓ Lemon wedges for serving
- ✓ Chopped fresh parsley for garnish (optional)

Method:

1. In a large bowl, whisk together the lemon zest, lemon juice, minced garlic, chopped rosemary, chopped thyme, olive oil, salt, and pepper to make the marinade.
2. Place the lamb chops in a shallow dish or resealable plastic bag and pour the marinade over them. Make sure the lamb chops are evenly coated. Cover the dish or seal the bag and refrigerate for at least 1 hour or overnight for best results.
3. Preheat the grill to medium-high heat.
4. Remove the lamb chops from the marinade and discard any excess marinade.
5. Grill the lamb chops on each side for 3-4 minutes for medium-rare or longer to reach your desired level of doneness.
6. Remove the lamb chops from the grill and let them rest for a few minutes before serving.

7. If desired, garnish with chopped fresh parsley and serve with lemon wedges on the side for squeezing over the lamb chops. Enjoy!

Lemon Poppy Seed Cake

Introduction: This Lemon Poppy Seed Cake is a delightful dessert perfect for any occasion. Moist and tender, with a bright lemon flavor and a hint of crunch from poppy seeds, it is sure to be a hit with lemon lovers everywhere.

Prep Time: 15 minutes Bake Time: 45 minutes Total Time: 1 hour

Ingredients:

- ✓ 1 1/2 cups all-purpose flour
- ✓ 2 tablespoons poppy seeds
- ✓ 1 teaspoon baking powder
- ✓ 1/2 teaspoon baking soda
- ✓ 1/4 teaspoon salt
- ✓ 1/2 cup unsalted butter, softened
- ✓ 1 cup granulated sugar
- ✓ 2 large eggs
- ✓ 1/2 cup Greek yogurt
- ✓ Zest and juice of 2 lemons
- ✓ 1 teaspoon vanilla extract
- ✓ Powdered sugar for dusting (optional)
- ✓ Lemon slices for garnish (optional)

Method:

1. Preheat the oven to 350°F (175°C). Grease and flour a 9x5 inch loaf pan.
2. whisk together the flour, poppy seeds, baking powder, baking soda, and salt in a medium bowl.
3. In a large bowl, cream the softened butter and granulated sugar until light and fluffy.
4. Beat in the eggs one at a time, then stir in the Greek yogurt, lemon zest, lemon juice, and vanilla extract until well combined.
5. Gradually add the dry ingredients to the wet ingredients, mixing until combined. Be careful not to overmix.
6. Pour the batter into the prepared loaf pan and spread it into an even layer.

7. Bake in the oven for 40-45 minutes or until a toothpick inserted into the center comes clean.
8. Remove the cake from the oven and let it cool in the pan for 10 minutes, then transfer it to a wire rack to cool completely.
9. Once cooled, dust the lemon poppy seed cake with powdered sugar before serving, if desired. Garnish with lemon slices for an extra touch. Enjoy!

Lemon Garlic Butter Zucchini Noodles

These Lemon Garlic Butter Zucchini Noodles are a light and flavorful alternative to traditional pasta. Spiralized zucchini noodles are tossed in a tangy lemon garlic butter sauce, resulting in a fresh, healthy, and delicious dish.

Prep Time: 10 minutes Cook Time: 10 minutes Total Time: 20 minutes

Ingredients:

- ✓ 4 medium zucchini
- ✓ 2 tablespoons unsalted butter
- ✓ 3 cloves garlic, minced
- ✓ Zest and juice of 1 lemon
- ✓ Salt and pepper to taste
- ✓ Chopped fresh parsley for garnish (optional)
- ✓ Grated Parmesan cheese for serving (optional)

Method:

1. Spiralize the zucchini into noodles using a spiralizer. Alternatively, a vegetable peeler can create long, thin strips.
2. Heat the butter in a large skillet over medium heat. Add the minced garlic and cook for 1-2 minutes or until fragrant.
3. Add the spiralized zucchini noodles to the skillet and toss to coat in the garlic butter sauce.
4. Cook for 3-5 minutes, stirring occasionally, until the zucchini noodles are tender.
5. Stir in the lemon zest and lemon juice, then season with salt and pepper to taste.
6. Remove from heat and transfer the zucchini noodles to a serving dish.
7. Garnish with chopped fresh parsley and grated Parmesan cheese, if desired.
8. Serve the lemon garlic butter zucchini noodles immediately as a light, flavorful side dish or main course. Enjoy!

Lemon Basil Chicken Salad

This Lemon Basil Chicken Salad is a light, refreshing dish perfect for a summertime lunch or dinner. Tender chicken breast is combined with crisp vegetables and fresh basil, then tossed in a zesty lemon dressing, creating a vibrant and flavorful salad that's sure to please.

Prep Time: 15 minutes Cook Time: 15 minutes Total Time: 30 minutes

Ingredients:

- ✓ 2 boneless, skinless chicken breasts
- ✓ Salt and pepper to taste
- ✓ 2 tablespoons olive oil
- ✓ Zest and juice of 1 lemon
- ✓ 2 tablespoons chopped fresh basil
- ✓ 2 cups mixed salad greens
- ✓ 1 cup cherry tomatoes, halved
- ✓ 1/2 English cucumber, diced
- ✓ 1/4 cup sliced red onion
- ✓ 1/4 cup crumbled feta cheese (optional)
- ✓ Lemon wedges for serving

Method:

1. Season the chicken breasts with salt and pepper to taste.
2. Heat the olive oil in a skillet over medium-high heat. Add the chicken breasts to the skillet and cook on each side for 6-7 minutes until they are cooked through and no longer pink in the center.
3. Remove the chicken breasts from the skillet and let them rest for a few minutes before slicing into strips.
4. To make the dressing, whisk together the lemon zest, lemon juice, and chopped fresh basil in a small bowl.
5. combine the mixed salad greens, cherry tomatoes, diced cucumber, sliced red onion, and sliced chicken breast strips in a large bowl.
6. Drizzle the lemon basil dressing over the salad and toss to coat evenly.

7. Divide the salad onto serving plates and sprinkle with crumbled feta cheese, if desired.
8. Serve the lemon basil chicken salad with lemon wedges on the side for squeezing over the salad. Enjoy!

Lemon Thyme Roasted Cauliflower

This lemon thyme roasted cauliflower is a simple yet flavorful side dish perfect for any meal. Tender cauliflower florets are roasted to golden perfection with aromatic thyme and zesty lemon, creating a comforting and elegant dish.

Prep Time: 10 minutes Cook Time: 25 minutes Total Time: 35 minutes

Ingredients:

- ✓ 1 head cauliflower, cut into florets
- ✓ 2 tablespoons olive oil
- ✓ Zest and juice of 1 lemon
- ✓ 2 teaspoons fresh thyme leaves
- ✓ Salt and pepper to taste
- ✓ Lemon wedges for serving

Method:

1. Preheat the oven to 425°F (220°C). Line a baking sheet with parchment paper.
2. In a large bowl, toss the cauliflower florets with olive oil, lemon zest, lemon juice, fresh thyme leaves, salt, and pepper until evenly coated.
3. Spread the seasoned cauliflower florets in a single layer on the prepared baking sheet.
4. Roast in the oven for 20-25 minutes, stirring halfway through, or until the cauliflower is tender and golden brown around the edges.
5. Remove from the oven and transfer the roasted cauliflower to a serving dish.
6. Serve the lemon thyme roasted cauliflower warm, with lemon wedges on the side for squeezing. Enjoy!

Lemon Ginger Turmeric Tea

This Lemon Ginger Turmeric Tea is a soothing and invigorating beverage perfect for any time of day. Made with fresh ginger, ground turmeric, and zesty lemon, it is not only delicious but also packed with immune-boosting properties and anti-inflammatory benefits.

Prep Time: 5 minutes Cook Time: 10 minutes Total Time: 15 minutes

Ingredients:

- ✓ 4 cups water
- ✓ 1-inch piece of fresh ginger, thinly sliced
- ✓ 1 teaspoon ground turmeric
- ✓ Zest and juice of 1 lemon
- ✓ Honey or maple syrup to taste (optional)

Method:

1. In a small saucepan, bring the water to a boil.
2. Add the sliced ginger and ground turmeric to the boiling water.
3. Reduce the heat to low and let the mixture simmer for 8-10 minutes.
4. Remove from heat and strain the tea into a teapot or serving pitcher.
5. Stir in the lemon zest and lemon juice.
6. Sweeten with honey or maple syrup to taste, if desired.
7. Pour the lemon ginger turmeric tea into mugs and serve hot.
8. Enjoy the comforting and immune-boosting benefits of this delightful tea!

Lemon Garlic Butter Roasted Corn

This Lemon Garlic Butter Roasted Corn is a simple, flavorful side dish perfect for summer gatherings and barbecues. Fresh corn on the cob is roasted with a tangy lemon garlic butter sauce, resulting in tender, caramelized kernels bursting with flavor.

Prep Time: 10 minutes Cook Time: 20 minutes Total Time: 30 minutes

Ingredients:

- ✓ 4 ears of corn, husked and cleaned
- ✓ 4 tablespoons unsalted butter, melted
- ✓ 2 cloves garlic, minced
- ✓ Zest and juice of 1 lemon
- ✓ Salt and pepper to taste
- ✓ Chopped fresh parsley for garnish (optional)

Method:

1. Preheat the oven to 400°F (200°C). Line a baking sheet with aluminum foil.
2. Place the cleaned ears of corn on the prepared baking sheet.
3. whisk together the melted butter, minced garlic, lemon zest, and lemon juice in a small bowl.
4. Brush the lemon garlic butter mixture over the ears of corn, coating them evenly.
5. Season the corn with salt and pepper to taste.
6. Roast the corn in the oven for 15-20 minutes, or until the kernels are tender and lightly browned, turning the ears halfway through cooking.
7. Remove from the oven and transfer the roasted corn to a serving platter.
8. Garnish with chopped fresh parsley, if desired, and serve immediately. Enjoy!

Lemon Blueberry Cheesecake

This Lemon Blueberry Cheesecake is a heavenly dessert combining tangy lemon and sweet blueberries in a rich and creamy cheesecake filling. With a buttery graham cracker crust and a luscious lemon-blueberry topping, this cheesecake is sure to impress at any gathering.

Prep Time: 30 minutes Chill Time: 4 hours Total Time: 4 hours 30 minutes

Ingredients:

For the Crust:

- ✓ 1 1/2 cups graham cracker crumbs
- ✓ 1/4 cup granulated sugar
- ✓ 1/2 cup unsalted butter, melted

For the Cheesecake Filling:

- ✓ 24 ounces cream cheese, softened
- ✓ 1 cup granulated sugar
- ✓ 3 large eggs
- ✓ 1 teaspoon vanilla extract
- ✓ Zest and juice of 2 lemons
- ✓ 1 cup fresh blueberries

For the Blueberry Topping:

- ✓ 1 cup fresh blueberries
- ✓ 1/4 cup granulated sugar
- ✓ 1 tablespoon lemon juice
- ✓ 1 teaspoon cornstarch
- ✓ 1 tablespoon water

Method:

1. Preheat the oven to 325°F (160°C). Grease a 9-inch springform pan and wrap the outside with aluminum foil to prevent leaks.

2. Mix the graham cracker crumbs, sugar, and melted butter in a medium bowl until well combined. Press the mixture into the bottom of the prepared springform pan.

3. In a large bowl, beat the softened cream cheese and sugar until smooth and creamy. Add the eggs one at a time, beating well after each addition. Stir in the vanilla extract, lemon zest, and lemon juice until fully incorporated.

4. Gently fold in the fresh blueberries.

5. Pour the cheesecake filling over the prepared crust in the springform pan, smoothing the top with a spatula.

6. Place the springform pan in a larger baking dish and add hot water to the larger dish until it reaches halfway up the sides of the springform pan.

7. Bake in the oven for 55-60 minutes or until the edges are set, but the center still jiggles slightly.

8. Turn off the oven and leave the cheesecake inside with the door slightly ajar for 1 hour to cool gradually.

9. Remove the cheesecake from the oven and refrigerate for at least 4 hours, until fully chilled and set.

10. Before serving, prepare the blueberry topping: In a small saucepan, combine the fresh blueberries, sugar, and lemon juice. Mix the cornstarch and water until smooth in a separate small bowl, then add it to the blueberry mixture. Cook over medium heat, stirring constantly, until the mixture thickens and the blueberries soften about 5 minutes. Remove from heat and let cool.

11. Once the cheesecake is chilled, carefully remove it from the springform pan and transfer it to a serving platter. Spoon the blueberry topping over the cheesecake.

12. Slice and serve the lemon blueberry cheesecake, and enjoy this delightful dessert!

Lemon Herb Baked Cod

This Lemon Herb Baked Cod is a light and flavorful dish perfect for a healthy dinner. Tender cod fillets are marinated in a zesty lemon herb mixture and then baked to perfection, resulting in moist and flaky fish bursting with flavor.

Prep Time: 10 minutes Marinating Time: 30 minutes Cook Time: 15 minutes Total Time: 55 minutes

Ingredients:

- ✓ 4 cod fillets
- ✓ Zest and juice of 1 lemon
- ✓ 2 tablespoons olive oil
- ✓ 2 cloves garlic, minced
- ✓ 1 tablespoon chopped fresh parsley
- ✓ 1 tablespoon chopped fresh dill
- ✓ Salt and pepper to taste
- ✓ Lemon slices for serving

Method:

1. In a small bowl, whisk together the lemon zest, lemon juice, olive oil, minced garlic, chopped parsley, chopped dill, salt, and pepper to make the marinade.
2. Place the cod fillets in a shallow dish or resealable plastic bag and pour the marinade over them, making sure they are evenly coated. Cover the dish or seal the bag and refrigerate for at least 30 minutes to allow the flavors to meld.
3. Preheat the oven to 400°F (200°C). Grease a baking dish or line it with parchment paper.
4. Remove the cod fillets from the marinade and place them in the prepared baking dish.
5. Bake in the oven for 12-15 minutes or until the fish is opaque and flakes easily with a fork.
6. Remove from the oven and let the baked cod rest for a few minutes before serving.

Lemon Ricotta Stuffed Shells

These Lemon Ricotta Stuffed Shells are a delightful twist on the classic stuffed pasta dish. Jumbo pasta shells are filled with a creamy mixture of ricotta cheese, spinach, and lemon zest, then baked to perfection with a tangy marinara sauce and melted mozzarella cheese.

Prep Time: 20 minutes Cook Time: 40 minutes Total Time: 1 hour

Ingredients:

- ✓ 1 box (12 ounces) jumbo pasta shells
- ✓ 2 cups ricotta cheese
- ✓ 1 cup grated Parmesan cheese, divided
- ✓ 1 cup chopped fresh spinach
- ✓ Zest of 1 lemon
- ✓ 1 egg
- ✓ 1 teaspoon garlic powder
- ✓ Salt and pepper to taste
- ✓ 2 cups marinara sauce
- ✓ 1 cup shredded mozzarella cheese
- ✓ Chopped fresh parsley for garnish (optional)
- ✓ Lemon wedges for serving

Method:

1. Preheat the oven to 375°F (190°C). Grease a 9x13-inch baking dish.
2. Cook the jumbo pasta shells according to the package instructions until al dente. Drain and set aside.
3. In a large bowl, mix the ricotta cheese, 1/2 cup of grated Parmesan cheese, chopped spinach, lemon zest, egg, garlic powder, salt, and pepper until well combined.
4. Spoon the ricotta mixture into the cooked pasta shells, filling each shell generously.
5. Spread a thin layer of marinara sauce on the bottom of the prepared baking dish. Arrange the stuffed shells in the dish in a single layer.
6. Cover the remaining marinara sauce over the stuffed shells evenly.

7. Sprinkle the shredded mozzarella cheese and the remaining 1/2 cup of grated Parmesan cheese over the top.
8. Cover the baking dish with aluminum foil and bake in the oven for 25 minutes.
9. Remove the foil and continue baking for 15 minutes until the cheese is melted and bubbly and the stuffed shells are heated through.
10. Remove from the oven and let the stuffed shells cool for a few minutes before serving.
11. If desired, garnish with chopped fresh parsley and serve with lemon wedges on the side for squeezing. Enjoy!

Lemon Basil Grilled Shrimp

These Lemon Basil Grilled Shrimp are a light and flavorful dish perfect for summer grilling. Jumbo shrimp are marinated in a tangy lemon-basil mixture and grilled to perfection, producing tender and juicy shrimp with fresh flavor in every bite.

Prep Time: 15 minutes Marinating Time: 30 minutes Cook Time: 6 minutes Total Time: 51 minutes

Ingredients:

- ✓ 1 pound jumbo shrimp, peeled and deveined
- ✓ Zest and juice of 1 lemon
- ✓ 2 tablespoons chopped fresh basil
- ✓ 2 cloves garlic, minced
- ✓ 2 tablespoons olive oil
- ✓ Salt and pepper to taste
- ✓ Lemon wedges for serving

Method:

1. In a large bowl, whisk together the lemon zest, lemon juice, chopped fresh basil, minced garlic, olive oil, salt, and pepper to make the marinade.
2. Add the peeled and deveined shrimp to the marinade, tossing to coat evenly. Cover the bowl and refrigerate for at least 30 minutes to allow the flavors to meld.
3. Preheat the grill to medium-high heat.
4. Thread the marinated shrimp onto skewers, dividing them evenly.
5. Grill the shrimp skewers on each side for 2-3 minutes until they are pink and opaque.
6. Remove from the grill and transfer the grilled shrimp skewers to a serving platter.
7. Serve the lemon basil grilled shrimp immediately with lemon wedges on the side for squeezing. Enjoy!

Lemon Garlic Butter Roasted Potatoes

These Lemon Garlic Butter Roasted Potatoes are a simple, flavorful side dish that pairs perfectly with any meal. Baby potatoes are roasted until crispy and golden brown, then tossed in a tangy lemon garlic butter sauce, resulting in tender potatoes on the inside and crispy on the outside with a fresh flavor.

Prep Time: 10 minutes Cook Time: 30 minutes Total Time: 40 minutes

Ingredients:

- ✓ 1 1/2 pounds baby potatoes, halved
- ✓ 3 tablespoons melted butter
- ✓ 3 cloves garlic, minced
- ✓ Zest and juice of 1 lemon
- ✓ 1 tablespoon chopped fresh parsley
- ✓ Salt and pepper to taste

Method:

Preheat the oven to 400°F (200°C). Line a baking sheet with parchment paper.

In a large bowl, toss the halved baby potatoes with melted butter, minced garlic, lemon zest, lemon juice, chopped fresh parsley, salt, and pepper until evenly coated.

Spread the seasoned potatoes in a single layer on the prepared baking sheet.

Roast in the preheated oven for 25-30 minutes, stirring halfway through, or until the potatoes are crispy and golden brown.

Remove from the oven and transfer the roasted potatoes to a serving dish.

Serve the lemon garlic butter roasted potatoes warm as a delicious side dish to complement any meal. Enjoy!

Lemon Glazed Donuts

These lemon-glazed donuts are a delightful treat that perfectly balances the tangy flavor of lemon with the sweetness of a classic donut. Light and fluffy donuts are dipped in a zesty lemon glaze, creating citrusy goodness in every bite.

Prep Time: 20 minutes Cook Time: 10 minutes Total Time: 30 minutes

Ingredients:

For the Donuts:

- ✓ 2 cups all-purpose flour
- ✓ 1/2 cup granulated sugar
- ✓ 1 tablespoon baking powder
- ✓ 1/2 teaspoon salt
- ✓ 3/4 cup milk
- ✓ 2 large eggs
- ✓ 2 tablespoons unsalted butter, melted
- ✓ Zest of 2 lemons
- ✓ 1 teaspoon vanilla extract

For the Lemon Glaze:

- ✓ 1 1/2 cups powdered sugar
- ✓ 3-4 tablespoons fresh lemon juice
- ✓ Zest of 1 lemon

Method:

1. Preheat the oven to 350°F (175°C). Grease a donut pan with non-stick cooking spray.
2. Whisk the flour, sugar, baking powder, and salt in a large mixing bowl.
3. In a separate bowl, whisk the milk, eggs, melted butter, lemon zest, and vanilla extract until well combined.
4. Pour the wet ingredients into the dry ingredients and stir until combined. Be careful not to overmix.

5. Spoon the batter into the prepared donut pan, filling each mold about 2/3 full.
6. Bake in the preheated oven for 8-10 minutes or until the donuts spring back when lightly touched.
7. Remove the donuts from the oven and let them cool in the pan for a few minutes before transferring them to a wire rack to cool completely.

For the Lemon Glaze:

1. In a medium bowl, whisk together the powdered sugar, fresh lemon juice, and lemon zest until smooth and well combined.
2. Dip each cooled donut into the lemon glaze, allowing any excess glaze to drip off.
3. Place the glazed donuts back on the wire rack to set for a few minutes.
4. Enjoy these delightful lemon-glazed donuts as a sweet treat for breakfast or dessert!

Lemon Raspberry Chia Pudding

This Lemon Raspberry Chia Pudding is a light, refreshing dessert or snack packed with flavor and nutrients. Creamy chia pudding infused with lemon zest and juice is layered with vibrant raspberry compote, creating a delicious and satisfying treat for any time of day.

Prep Time: 10 minutes Chilling Time: 2 hours Total Time: 2 hours 10 minutes

Ingredients:

For the Chia Pudding:

- ✓ 1/4 cup chia seeds
- ✓ 1 cup almond milk (or any milk of choice)
- ✓ Zest of 1 lemon
- ✓ 2 tablespoons fresh lemon juice
- ✓ 2 tablespoons maple syrup or honey

For the Raspberry Compote:

- ✓ 1 cup fresh or frozen raspberries
- ✓ 2 tablespoons maple syrup or honey
- ✓ 1 tablespoon water
- ✓ 1 teaspoon lemon juice

Method:

1. In a medium bowl, whisk together the chia seeds, almond milk, lemon zest, lemon juice, and maple syrup (or honey) until well combined.
2. Cover the bowl and refrigerate for at least 2 hours, or overnight, to allow the chia seeds to gel and thicken.
3. combine the raspberries, maple syrup (or honey), water, and lemon juice in a small saucepan. Cook over medium heat, stirring occasionally, until the raspberries break down and the mixture thickens slightly about 5-7 minutes. Remove from heat and let cool.
4. To assemble, evenly divide the chilled chia pudding among serving glasses or jars.

5. Spoon the raspberry compote over the top of each serving of chia pudding.
6. Garnish with additional lemon zest or fresh raspberries, if desired.
7. Serve the lemon raspberry chia pudding chilled, and enjoy this nutritious and delicious treat!

Lemon Rosemary Grilled Pork Chops

These Lemon Rosemary Grilled Pork Chops are a delicious and flavorful dish perfect for a summer barbecue. Thick-cut pork chops are marinated in a tangy lemon-rosemary mixture and grilled to perfection, producing juicy and tender chops with fresh flavor in every bite.

Prep Time: 10 minutes Marinating Time: 1-2 hours Cook Time: 10 minutes Total Time: 1 hour 20 minutes

Ingredients:

- ✓ 4 bone-in pork chops
- ✓ Zest and juice of 2 lemons
- ✓ 2 tablespoons olive oil
- ✓ 2 cloves garlic, minced
- ✓ 1 tablespoon chopped fresh rosemary
- ✓ Salt and pepper to taste
- ✓ Lemon wedges for serving

Method:

1. whisk together the lemon zest, lemon juice, olive oil, minced garlic, chopped fresh rosemary, salt, and pepper in a small bowl to make the marinade.
2. Place the pork chops in a shallow dish or resealable plastic bag and pour the marinade over them. Make sure the pork chops are evenly coated. Cover the dish or seal the bag and refrigerate for 1-2 hours to allow the flavors to meld.
3. Preheat the grill to medium-high heat.
4. Remove the pork chops from the marinade and discard any excess marinade.
5. Grill the pork chops for 4-5 minutes on each side or until they are cooked through and have reached an internal temperature of 145°F (63°C).
6. Remove from the grill and let the pork chops rest for a few minutes before serving.
7. Serve the lemon rosemary grilled pork chops with lemon wedges.

Lemon Garlic Butter Green Peas

These Lemon Garlic Butter Green Peas are a simple yet flavorful side dish that pairs perfectly with various main courses. Tender green peas are sautéed in a tangy lemon garlic butter sauce, creating a vibrant and delicious addition to any meal.

Prep Time: 5 minutes Cook Time: 10 minutes Total Time: 15 minutes

Ingredients:

- ✓ 2 cups frozen green peas
- ✓ 2 tablespoons unsalted butter
- ✓ 2 cloves garlic, minced
- ✓ Zest and juice of 1 lemon
- ✓ Salt and pepper to taste
- ✓ Chopped fresh parsley for garnish (optional)

Method:

1. In a medium saucepan, bring water to a boil. Add the frozen green peas and cook for 3-4 minutes or until tender but still vibrant green. Drain and set aside.
2. Melt the butter in the same saucepan over medium heat. Add the minced garlic and cook for 1-2 minutes, or until fragrant.
3. Add the cooked green peas to the saucepan with the garlic butter mixture.
4. Add the lemon zest and juice to the peas and toss to coat evenly.
5. Season with salt and pepper to taste.
6. Cook for 2-3 minutes, stirring occasionally, until the peas are heated and coated in the lemon garlic butter sauce.
7. Remove from heat and transfer the green peas to a serving dish.
8. If desired, garnish with chopped fresh parsley and serve immediately as a delicious side dish. Enjoy!

Lemon Pepper Roasted Chickpeas

These lemon pepper-roasted chickpeas are a crunchy and flavorful snack perfect for munching on the go or adding to salads and bowls. Canned chickpeas are seasoned with zesty lemon and spicy pepper, then roasted until crispy, creating a satisfying and nutritious treat.

Prep Time: 5 minutes Cook Time: 30 minutes Total Time: 35 minutes

Ingredients:

- ✓ 1 can (15 ounces) chickpeas (garbanzo beans), drained and rinsed
- ✓ 2 tablespoons olive oil
- ✓ Zest of 1 lemon
- ✓ 1 teaspoon ground black pepper
- ✓ 1/2 teaspoon salt
- ✓ 1/2 teaspoon garlic powder
- ✓ 1/4 teaspoon cayenne pepper (optional)

Method:

1. Preheat the oven to 400°F (200°C). Line a baking sheet with parchment paper.
2. Pat the rinsed chickpeas dry with paper towels to remove excess moisture.
3. In a mixing bowl, combine the dried chickpeas, olive oil, lemon zest, ground black pepper, salt, garlic powder, and cayenne pepper (if using). Toss until the chickpeas are evenly coated.
4. Spread the seasoned chickpeas in a single layer on the prepared baking sheet.
5. Roast in the preheated oven for 25-30 minutes, stirring halfway through, or until the chickpeas are golden brown and crispy.
6. Remove the roasted chickpeas from the oven and let them cool on the baking sheet for a few minutes.
7. Transfer the chickpeas to a serving bowl and let them cool completely before serving.
8. Enjoy these lemon pepper roasted chickpeas as a crunchy snack or a topping for salads and bowls!

Lemon Basil Orzo Salad

This Lemon Basil Orzo Salad is a light, refreshing dish perfect for summer gatherings and picnics. Cooked orzo pasta is tossed with fresh basil, cherry tomatoes, and a zesty lemon dressing, creating a vibrant and flavorful salad that's sure to impress.

Prep Time: 10 minutes Cook Time: 10 minutes Total Time: 20 minutes

Ingredients:

- ✓ 1 cup orzo pasta
- ✓ 2 cups cherry tomatoes, halved
- ✓ 1/4 cup chopped fresh basil
- ✓ Zest and juice of 1 lemon
- ✓ 2 tablespoons extra virgin olive oil
- ✓ 1 clove garlic, minced
- ✓ Salt and pepper to taste
- ✓ Grated Parmesan cheese for garnish (optional)

Method:

1. Cook the orzo pasta according to the package instructions until al dente. Drain and rinse under cold water to stop the cooking process. Drain well.
2. combine the cooked orzo pasta, halved cherry tomatoes, and chopped fresh basil in a large mixing bowl.
3. To make the dressing, whisk together the lemon zest, lemon juice, extra virgin olive oil, minced garlic, salt, and pepper in a small bowl.
4. Pour the dressing over the orzo salad and toss until everything is evenly coated.
5. Taste and adjust the seasoning, if necessary.
6. Transfer the orzo salad to a serving dish and garnish with grated Parmesan cheese, if desired.
7. Serve the lemon basil orzo salad chilled or at room temperature, and enjoy this delightful summer dish!

Lemon Garlic Butter Spaghetti Squash

This Lemon Garlic Butter Spaghetti Squash is a healthier alternative to traditional pasta dishes. Roasted spaghetti squash strands are tossed in a tangy lemon garlic butter sauce, creating a delicious and satisfying meal for a light lunch or dinner.

Prep Time: 10 minutes Cook Time: 40 minutes Total Time: 50 minutes

Ingredients:

- ✓ 1 medium spaghetti squash
- ✓ 2 tablespoons unsalted butter
- ✓ 2 cloves garlic, minced
- ✓ Zest and juice of 1 lemon
- ✓ Salt and pepper to taste
- ✓ Chopped fresh parsley for garnish (optional)
- ✓ Grated Parmesan cheese for serving (optional)

Method:

1. Preheat the oven to 400°F (200°C). Line a baking sheet with parchment paper.
2. Carefully cut the spaghetti squash in half lengthwise using a sharp knife. Scoop out the seeds and discard them.
3. Place the squash halves, cut side down, on the prepared baking sheet.
4. Roast in the oven for 35-40 minutes or until the squash is tender and easily pierced with a fork.
5. While the squash is roasting, melt the butter in a small saucepan over medium heat. Add the minced garlic and cook for 1-2 minutes or until fragrant.
6. Stir in the lemon zest and juice, and season with salt and pepper to taste. Remove from heat and set aside.
7. Once the squash is done roasting, remove it from the oven and let it cool for a few minutes.
8. Use a fork to scrape the flesh of the squash into spaghetti-like strands and transfer them to a large mixing bowl.

9. Pour the lemon garlic butter sauce over the spaghetti squash strands and toss until evenly coated.
10. Transfer the dressed spaghetti squash to serving plates or bowls.
11. Garnish with chopped fresh parsley and grated Parmesan cheese, if desired.
12. Serve the lemon garlic butter spaghetti squash immediately as a delicious and nutritious meal. Enjoy!

Lemon Coconut Cupcakes

These Lemon Coconut Cupcakes are a delightful combination of tangy lemon and sweet coconut flavors. Moist and fluffy lemon cupcakes are topped with creamy coconut frosting, creating a delicious treat for any occasion.

Prep Time: 20 minutes Cook Time: 20 minutes Total Time: 40 minutes

Ingredients:

For the Lemon Cupcakes:

- ✓ 1 1/2 cups all-purpose flour
- ✓ 1 1/2 teaspoons baking powder
- ✓ 1/4 teaspoon salt
- ✓ 1/2 cup unsalted butter, softened
- ✓ 3/4 cup granulated sugar
- ✓ 2 large eggs
- ✓ Zest and juice of 1 lemon
- ✓ 1/2 cup milk
- ✓ 1 teaspoon vanilla extract

For the Coconut Frosting:

- ✓ 1/2 cup unsalted butter, softened
- ✓ 2 cups powdered sugar
- ✓ 1/4 cup coconut milk
- ✓ 1/2 teaspoon coconut extract
- ✓ 1/2 cup shredded coconut, toasted (for garnish)

Method:

1. Preheat the oven to 350°F (175°C). Line a muffin tin with cupcake liners.
2. whisk together the flour, baking powder, and salt in a medium bowl. Set aside.
3. In a large mixing bowl, cream the softened butter and granulated sugar until light and fluffy.

4. Beat in the eggs, one at a time, until well combined. Stir in the lemon zest and lemon juice.
5. Gradually add the dry ingredients to the wet ingredients, alternating with the milk, beginning and ending with the dry ingredients. Mix until just combined. Stir in the vanilla extract.
6. Divide the batter evenly among the prepared cupcake liners, filling each about 2/3 full.
7. Bake in the preheated oven for 18-20 minutes or until a toothpick inserted into the center of a cupcake comes out clean.
8. Remove the cupcakes from the oven and let them cool in the muffin tin for a few minutes before transferring them to a wire rack to cool completely.
9. While the cupcakes are cooling, prepare the coconut frosting. In a mixing bowl, beat the softened butter until smooth and creamy. Gradually add the powdered sugar, coconut milk, and coconut extract, and beat until light and fluffy.
10. Once the cupcakes are completely cool, frost them with the coconut frosting using a piping bag or offset spatula.
11. Sprinkle the toasted shredded coconut over the frosted cupcakes for garnish.
12. Serve these lemon coconut cupcakes and enjoy these delightful treats!

Lemon Herb Roasted Chicken Thighs

These Lemon Herb-Roasted Chicken Thighs are a simple and delicious main dish that's perfect for a family dinner or gathering. Bone-in chicken thighs are marinated in a zesty lemon herb mixture and roasted to juicy perfection, resulting in flavorful and tender chicken thighs that everyone will love.

Prep Time: 10 minutes Marinating Time: 30 minutes Cook Time: 35 minutes Total Time: 1 hour 15 minutes

Ingredients:

- ✓ 6 bone-in, skin-on chicken thighs
- ✓ Zest and juice of 2 lemons
- ✓ 3 cloves garlic, minced
- ✓ 2 tablespoons olive oil
- ✓ 1 tablespoon chopped fresh rosemary
- ✓ 1 tablespoon chopped fresh thyme
- ✓ Salt and pepper to taste
- ✓ Lemon slices for serving

Method:

1. In a small bowl, whisk together the lemon zest, lemon juice, minced garlic, olive oil, chopped fresh rosemary, chopped fresh thyme, salt, and pepper to make the marinade.
2. Place the chicken thighs in a shallow dish or resealable plastic bag and pour the marinade over them, making sure they are evenly coated. Cover the dish or seal the bag and refrigerate for at least 30 minutes to allow the flavors to meld.
3. Preheat the oven to 425°F (220°C). Line a baking sheet with parchment paper.
4. Remove the chicken thighs from the marinade and arrange them skin-side on the prepared baking sheet.
5. Roast in the preheated oven for 30-35 minutes, or until the chicken thighs are golden brown and cooked through and have an internal temperature of 165°F (74°C).

6. Remove from the oven and let the chicken thighs rest for a few minutes before serving.

7. Serve the lemon herb roasted chicken thighs with lemon slices on the side for squeezing. Enjoy this flavorful and comforting dish!

Lemon Garlic Butter Mushrooms

Lemon Garlic Butter Mushrooms are a flavorful side dish that pairs perfectly with grilled meats or as a topping for pasta or rice dishes. Tender mushrooms are sautéed in a tangy lemon garlic butter sauce, creating a delicious and versatile dish that's quick and easy to prepare.

Prep Time: 10 minutes Cook Time: 10 minutes Total Time: 20 minutes

Ingredients:

- ✓ 1 pound mushrooms, cleaned and sliced
- ✓ 2 tablespoons unsalted butter
- ✓ 2 cloves garlic, minced
- ✓ Zest and juice of 1 lemon
- ✓ Salt and pepper to taste
- ✓ Chopped fresh parsley for garnish (optional)

Method:

1. Heat a large skillet over medium heat. Add the butter and let it melt.
2. Add the minced garlic to the skillet and sauté for 1-2 minutes or until fragrant.
3. Add the sliced mushrooms to the skillet and sauté for 5-7 minutes, stirring occasionally, until the mushrooms are tender and golden brown.
4. Stir in the lemon zest and juice, and season with salt and pepper to taste. Cook for 2-3 minutes, allowing the flavors to meld.
5. Remove from heat and transfer the lemon garlic butter mushrooms to a serving dish.
6. Garnish with chopped fresh parsley, if desired.
7. Serve the lemon garlic butter mushrooms hot as a delicious side dish or topping. Enjoy!

Lemon Poppy Seed Waffles

These Lemon Poppy Seed Waffles are a delightful twist on traditional waffles. They have the bright flavor of lemon and the crunch of poppy seeds. Crispy on the outside and fluffy on the inside, they are perfect for a leisurely weekend breakfast or brunch.

Prep Time: 10 minutes Cook Time: 15 minutes Total Time: 25 minutes

Ingredients:

- ✓ 2 cups all-purpose flour
- ✓ 1/4 cup granulated sugar
- ✓ 1 tablespoon baking powder
- ✓ 1/2 teaspoon baking soda
- ✓ 1/2 teaspoon salt
- ✓ Zest of 2 lemons
- ✓ 2 tablespoons poppy seeds
- ✓ 2 large eggs
- ✓ 1 3/4 cups buttermilk
- ✓ 1/2 cup unsalted butter, melted
- ✓ 2 tablespoons fresh lemon juice
- ✓ 1 teaspoon vanilla extract

Method:

1. Preheat your waffle iron according to the manufacturer's instructions.
2. Whisk the flour, sugar, baking powder, baking soda, salt, lemon zest, and poppy seeds in a large mixing bowl.
3. In a separate bowl, beat the eggs until light and frothy. Stir in the buttermilk, melted butter, lemon juice, and vanilla extract.
4. Pour the wet ingredients into the dry ingredients and stir until combined. Do not overmix; it's okay if the batter is slightly lumpy.
5. Ladle the batter onto the preheated waffle iron and cook according to the manufacturer's instructions until the waffles are golden brown and crisp.

6. Remove the cooked waffles from the iron and keep warm while you cook the remaining batter.
7. Warm the lemon poppy seed waffles with your favorite toppings, such as maple syrup, fresh berries, whipped cream, or lemon curd. Enjoy!

Lemon Herb Grilled Vegetable Skewers

These Lemon Herb Grilled Vegetable Skewers are a colorful and flavorful side dish perfect for summer barbecues or outdoor gatherings. Assorted vegetables are marinated in a zesty lemon herb dressing, threaded onto skewers, and grilled to perfection, resulting in tender and delicious veggies with a burst of fresh flavor.

Prep Time: 20 minutes Marinating Time: 30 minutes Cook Time: 10 minutes Total Time: 1 hour

Ingredients:

- ✓ 2 zucchinis, sliced into rounds
- ✓ 2 bell peppers (assorted colors), cut into chunks
- ✓ 1 red onion, cut into chunks
- ✓ 1 pint of cherry tomatoes
- ✓ Zest and juice of 2 lemons
- ✓ 1/4 cup olive oil
- ✓ 2 cloves garlic, minced
- ✓ 1 tablespoon chopped fresh basil
- ✓ 1 tablespoon chopped fresh parsley
- ✓ 1 teaspoon chopped fresh thyme
- ✓ Salt and pepper to taste
- ✓ Wooden skewers, soaked in water for 30 minutes

Method:

1. In a large mixing bowl, whisk together the lemon zest, lemon juice, olive oil, minced garlic, chopped fresh basil, chopped fresh parsley, chopped fresh thyme, salt, and pepper to make the marinade.
2. Add the sliced zucchini, bell pepper chunks, red onion chunks, and cherry tomatoes to the bowl with the marinade. Toss until the vegetables are evenly coated.
3. Cover the bowl and let the vegetables marinate in the refrigerator for at least 30 minutes, allowing the flavors to meld.
4. Preheat the grill to medium-high heat.

5. Thread the marinated vegetables onto the soaked wooden skewers, alternating between different vegetables.
6. Grill the vegetable skewers for 8-10 minutes, turning occasionally or until the vegetables are tender and lightly charred.
7. Remove from the grill and transfer the vegetable skewers to a serving platter.
8. Serve the lemon herb grilled vegetable skewers hot as a delicious and colorful side dish. Enjoy!

Made in the USA
Monee, IL
26 November 2024

71301306R00046